AUSTRALIA
TRAVEL GUIDE 2024;
EXPLORING THE BEST OF AUSTRALIA ON LOW BUDGET.

BEN CARTER

Reserved rights. Without the publisher's prior written consent, no part of this book may be duplicated, copied, or communicated in any way, including by photocopying, recording, or other electronic or mechanical techniques, unless expressly authorized by copyright laws.

TABLE OF CONTENTS

Chapter 1: Introduction 14
    Overview of Australia: 15
    Purpose of the Trip: 16

Chapter 2: Preparing for the Journey: 18
    Visa Requirements: 19
    Vaccinations and Health Precautions: 20
    Packing Essentials: 22

Chapter 3: Destinations in Australia: Sydney 24
    Opera House and Sydney Harbour: 25
        Bondi Beach: 26
        Taronga Zoo: 27
    Destinations in Australia: Melbourne 29
        Federation Square: 30

- Great Ocean Road: 30
- Royal Botanic Gardens: 32
- Destinations in Australia: Cairns 33
  - Great Barrier Reef: 34
  - Daintree Rainforest: 35
  - Kuranda Scenic Railway: 35

Chapter 4: Travel Logistics: Transportation within Australia. 37
- Domestic Flights: 38
  - Trains: 39
  - Buses and Coaches: 39
  - Public Transport in Cities: 40
  - Ride-Sharing Services: 41
  - Ferries: 41

Chapter 5: Accommodation Options 42
- Hotels and Resorts: 42
  - Hostels 43
  - Short-Term Rentals: 43
  - Motels and Motor Inns: 44
  - Bed and Breakfasts (B&Bs): 44
  - Currency and Banking: 44
  - Currency: 45
  - Banking: 45
  - Tipping: 46

Chapter 6: Australian Cuisine and Dining 47

Iconic Australian Dishes 47

- Vegemite on Toast: 48
- Tim Tam Slam: 48
- Pavlova: 48
- Meat Pie: 49
- Damper: 49
- Lamingtons: 50
- Kangaroo Steak: 50
- Flat White: 51
- Barramundi: 51

Chapter 7: Local Food Markets: 52

Queen Victoria Market (Melbourne): 53

- Sydney Fish Market (Sydney) 54
- Eumundi Markets (Queensland) 54
- Salamanca Market (Hobart) 54
- Fremantle Markets (Perth) 55

Dining Etiquette 55

- Tipping: 56
- Reservations: 56
- Table Service: 56
- Cutlery Usage 56
- Wine and Beer 57

Wait for the Host 57
Casual Atmosphere 57

Chapter 8: Cultural Experiences 58

Indigenous Australian Culture 58
    Indigenous Art 59
    Cultural Festivals and Events 59
    Cultural Centers and Museums 59
    Dreamtime Stories 60
    Guided Indigenous Tours: 60
    Artisan Markets: 61

Acknowledgment of Country: 61
    Bush Walks and Cultural Experiences: 61
    Language Workshops: 62
    Respectful Engagement 62

Festivals and Events: 63
    Sydney Festival (Sydney, NSW): 64
    Melbourne International Comedy Festival (Melbourne, VIC): 64
    Vivid Sydney (Sydney, NSW): 64
    WOMADelaide (Adelaide, SA): 65
    Woodford Folk Festival (Woodford, QLD): 65
    Museums and Galleries: 65
    National Gallery of Australia (Canberra, ACT): 66

    Art Gallery of New South Wales (Sydney, NSW): 66

    National Museum of Australia (Canberra, ACT): 67

    Museum of Old and New Art (MONA) (Hobart, TAS): ... 67

    Queensland Art Gallery and Gallery of Modern Art (Brisbane, QLD): 67

    Australian Museum (Sydney, NSW): 68

    Heide Museum of Modern Art (Melbourne, VIC): 68

Chapter 9: Adventure and Outdoor Activities....................... 69

    Hiking in the Blue Mountains 69

        Three Sisters and Echo Point: 70

        National Pass Trail: 70

        Wentworth Falls Track: 70

        Govetts Leap to Pulpit Rock: 71

        Grand Canyon Track: 71

        National Pass and Wentworth Falls Circuit: 71

        Sublime Point Lookout to Leura Cascades: 72

        Tips for Hiking in the Blue Mountains: 72

    Surfing in Byron Bay: 73

        Main Beach: 74

        The Pass: 74

        Wategos Beach: 74

        Tallow Beach: 75

        Surf Schools: 75

- Surfing Events: 76
- Sunrise Surf Sessions: 76
- Wildlife Encounters: 76
  - Whale Watching: 77
  - Cape Byron Walking Track: 77
  - Byron Bay Wildlife Sanctuary: 77
  - Dolphin Kayaking Tours: 78
  - Night Vision Walks: 78

Chapter 10: Practical Tips for Travelers: 80

- Voltage and Plugs: 80
  - Emergency Services: 81
  - Health Insurance: 81
  - Transportation Cards: 81
  - Sun Protection: 81
  - Currency Exchange: 82
  - Wi-Fi and SIM Cards: 82
  - Water Safety: 82
- Time Zones and Weather: 83
  - Time Zones: 83
  - Weather: 83
  - Diverse Climates: 83
  - Rainfall: 84
  - Packing Essentials: 84

Check Local Forecasts: 84

Chapter 11: Safety Tips: 86

Emergency Services: 86

Health Precautions: 87

Wildlife Caution: 87

Water Safety: 87

Sun Protection: 88

Weather Preparedness: 88

Transportation Safety: 88

Respect Local Customs: 89

Communication and Connectivity: 89

Mobile Networks: 89

Wi-Fi Availability: 90

Emergency Contact Information: 90

Navigation Apps: 90

Emergency Alerts: 91

Communication Language: 91

Internet Cafes: 91

Chapter 12: Sustainable Travel Practices 92

Reduce Single-Use Plastics: 93

Stay in Eco-Friendly Accommodations: 93

Conserve Water and Energy: 93

Support Local Products and Markets: 94

- Respect Wildlife: 94
- Responsible Tourism: 94
- Mindful Transportation: 95
- Leave No Trace: 95

Eco-friendly Activities: 95
- Nature Conservation Tours: 95
- Snorkeling in Marine Protected Areas: 96
- National Park Exploration: 96
- Bird Watching and Wildlife Safaris: 96
- Community-Based Tourism: 97
- Sustainable Food Experiences: 97
- Educational Eco-Tours: 97
- Volunteer Opportunities: 98

Responsible Wildlife Tourism: 99
- Choose Accredited Sanctuaries: 99
- No Interference with Wild Animals: 100
- Wildlife Conservation Tours: 100
- Avoid Selfies with Wildlife: 100
- Say No to Animal Performances: 101

Educate Yourself: 101
- Responsible Snorkeling and Diving: 101
- Report Unethical Practices: 102

Reduce, Reuse, Recycle: 102

Reduce Single-Use Plastics: 102
Choose Eco-Friendly Accommodations: 102
Pack Light and Wisely: 103
Use Public Transportation: 103
Support Sustainable Products: 103
Dispose of Waste Properly: 104
Conserve Water and Energy: 104
Participate in Clean-Up Initiatives: 104

What to see & do in United Arab Emirates

The choice of things to do in the United Arab Emirates is very impressive, thanks to the country's incredible variety of landscapes.

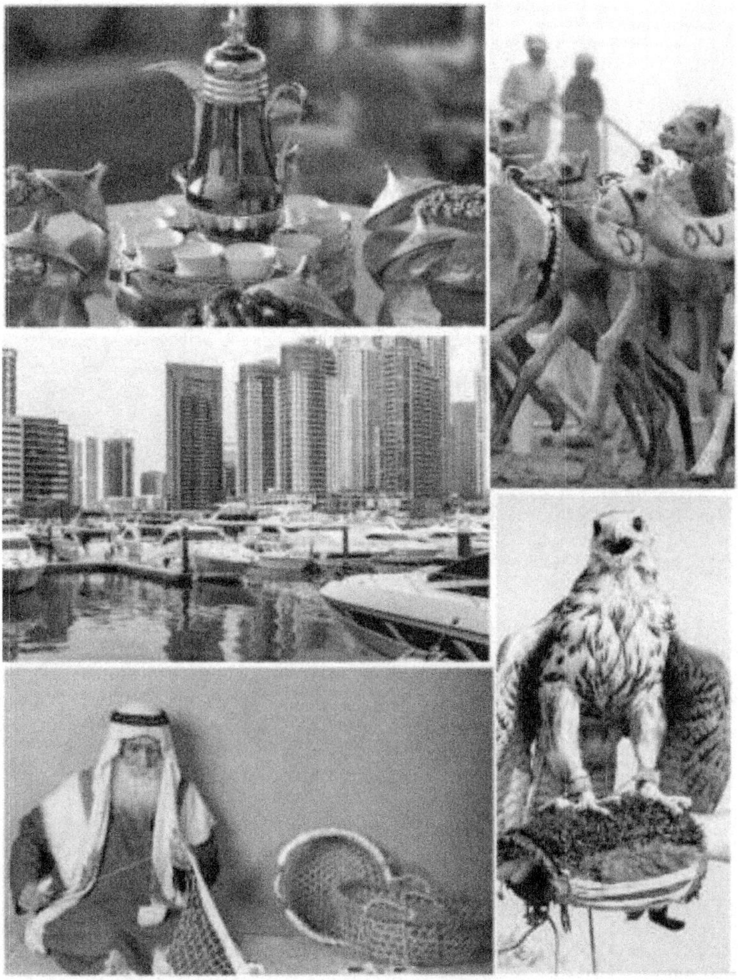

Chapter 1: Introduction

Australia, the world's sixth-largest country, is a vast and diverse land known for its unique wildlife, stunning landscapes, and vibrant cities. This introduction aims to set the stage for an unforgettable journey through this continent-country, providing a glimpse into the various facets that make Australia a sought-after destination for travelers.

Overview of Australia

Situated in the Southern Hemisphere, Australia boasts a diverse range of geographical features, from the iconic Sydney Opera House and the Great Barrier Reef to the vast Outback and ancient rainforests. Its cities, including Sydney, Melbourne, and Brisbane, offer a blend of modern urban living and rich cultural experiences. The unique flora and fauna, much of which is found nowhere else on Earth, contribute to Australia's distinct identity.

Australia's Aboriginal heritage, spanning thousands of years, adds a profound layer to its cultural landscape. Understanding the historical and cultural significance of the land enhances the travel experience, providing insights into the world's oldest continuous cultures.

Purpose of the Trip

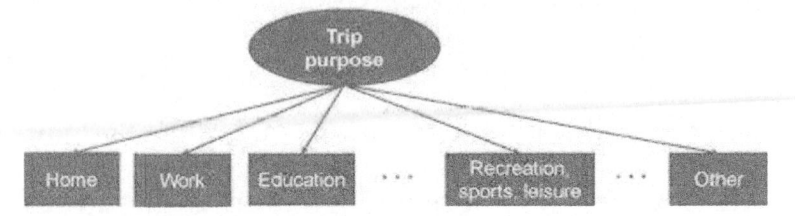

```
              Trip
            purpose
   ┌──────┬────┼────────┬──────┐
  Home  Work Education ... Recreation, ... Other
                          sports, leisure
```

The purpose of embarking on a journey to Australia can vary greatly among travelers. For some, it may be a quest for adventure, exploring the rugged terrains of the Outback or diving into the mesmerizing depths of the Great Barrier Reef. Others may seek cultural enrichment, delving into the indigenous heritage and contemporary arts scene.

Australia also appeals to those in search of relaxation, with its pristine beaches, tranquil landscapes, and world-class resorts offering a perfect escape from the hustle and bustle of everyday life. Whether the purpose is to witness the vibrant city life, explore natural wonders, or immerse oneself in cultural experiences, Australia offers a diverse array of activities and attractions to fulfill the desires of any traveler.

Chapter 2: Preparing for the Journey:

Embarking on a journey to Australia requires careful preparation to ensure a smooth and enjoyable experience. This section covers crucial aspects, starting with understanding and meeting visa requirements. Travelers must research the specific visa type required based on the purpose and duration of their stay. This could range from a tourist visa for a short visit to more specialized visas for work or study.

Visa Requirements

Australia has strict visa regulations, and obtaining the correct visa is essential. Travelers should check the official Australian government website or consult with the nearest Australian embassy or consulate for the most up-to-date information. Ensuring all necessary documents are in order and applying well in advance can prevent last-minute complications.

Vaccinations and Health Precautions

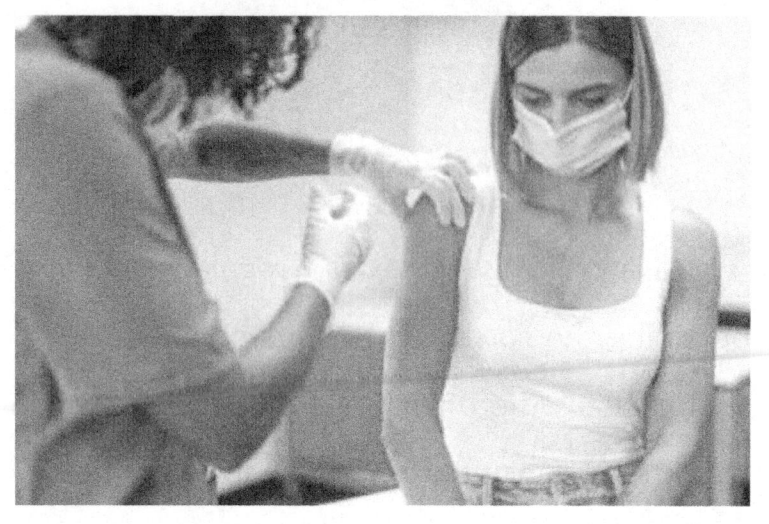

Before traveling to Australia, it is crucial to be aware of any required vaccinations and health precautions. Depending on the traveler's origin and recent travel history, certain vaccinations may be mandatory. Additionally, Australia's unique wildlife and environment mean that travelers should be aware of potential health risks, such as insect bites or exposure to extreme temperatures. Seeking advice from a healthcare professional and staying updated on health alerts will contribute to a safe and healthy journey.

Packing Essentials

Packing for a trip to Australia requires thoughtful consideration of the diverse climates and activities one might encounter. Essentials include lightweight clothing for the warm coastal areas, sturdy shoes for exploring natural landscapes, and layers for cooler evenings. Sun protection items like sunscreen, hats, and sunglasses are crucial due to the intense Australian sun.

Depending on the planned activities, packing items such as swimwear, hiking gear, and adapters for electronic devices is advisable.

It's also important to pack any necessary medications, a basic first aid kit, and a photocopy of important documents like passports and travel insurance. Adhering to airline baggage regulations and considering the baggage weight limits is essential to avoid any inconveniences during the journey.

Chapter 3: Destinations in Australia: Sydney

Sydney, the vibrant capital of New South Wales, offers a myriad of iconic attractions and experiences that capture the essence of Australia's urban and coastal charm.

Opera House and Sydney Harbour

The Sydney Opera House, a UNESCO World Heritage Site, stands as a symbol of architectural brilliance. Nestled against the backdrop of the stunning Sydney Harbour, it's not only an architectural marvel but also a hub for world-class performances. Exploring the Opera House's interior reveals its intricate design and cultural significance.

Adjacent to the Opera House, Sydney Harbour Bridge provides breathtaking panoramic views of the city. Visitors can choose to climb the bridge for an exhilarating experience or simply enjoy the scenery from the waterfront.

Bondi Beach:

For those seeking sun, surf, and a laid-back atmosphere, Bondi Beach is a must-visit destination. This iconic stretch of golden sand is a haven for surfers, swimmers, and beach lovers alike. The Bondi to Coogee coastal walk offers a scenic trek with stunning ocean views, passing by secluded coves and rock pools.

The vibrant Bondi Beach community is known for its diverse dining scene, from casual beachside cafes to upscale restaurants. Bondi also hosts numerous events and festivals throughout the year, adding to its lively atmosphere.

Taronga Zoo:

Situated on the shores of Sydney Harbour, Taronga Zoo provides a unique wildlife experience with a backdrop of the city skyline. Home to a diverse range of native and exotic animals, the zoo offers immersive exhibits and opportunities for up-close encounters.

Taronga Zoo's commitment to conservation and education enhances the visitor experience, making it an ideal destination for families and wildlife enthusiasts. The Sky Safari cable car provides not only a convenient way to navigate the zoo but also stunning views of Sydney Harbour.

Destinations in Australia

Melbourne

Melbourne, known for its artsy vibe, diverse culture, and culinary delights, beckons travelers with a mix of urban sophistication and natural wonders.

Federation Square:

Located at the heart of Melbourne, Federation Square serves as a cultural hub and meeting place. The distinctive architecture of the square, combined with its dynamic events and festivals, reflects Melbourne's commitment to the arts. Visitors can explore galleries, theaters, and cafes, making Federation Square a central point to immerse oneself in the city's creative energy.

Great Ocean Road:

A scenic drive along the Great Ocean Road is a quintessential Australian experience. Stretching along the southern coast, this road trip unveils breathtaking landscapes, including the iconic Twelve Apostles, limestone stacks rising from the Southern Ocean. The journey is punctuated with coastal cliffs, lush rainforests, and charming seaside villages, offering a diverse range of natural beauty.

Exploring the Great Ocean Road provides opportunities for outdoor activities, such as hiking and surfing, and allows travelers to witness the rugged splendor of Australia's coastline. Sunset at the Twelve Apostles is a particularly enchanting spectacle.

Royal Botanic Gardens

For a tranquil escape within the bustling city, Melbourne's Royal Botanic Gardens offers a haven of greenery and botanical wonders. Spanning vast acres, the gardens showcase a diverse collection of plants from around the world. Visitors can stroll through themed gardens, including the Australian Rainforest Walk and the Herb Garden.

The Royal Botanic Gardens also host cultural events, guided tours, and educational programs. The peaceful surroundings make it an ideal spot for a leisurely picnic or a quiet retreat from the urban buzz.

Destinations in Australia

Cairns

Cairns, a tropical paradise in Far North Queensland, serves as a gateway to some of

Australia's most spectacular natural wonders, offering a perfect blend of marine beauty and lush rainforest landscapes.

Great Barrier Reef:

Cairns is synonymous with the Great Barrier Reef, the world's largest coral reef system. A UNESCO World Heritage site, the reef is a marine wonderland teeming with vibrant coral formations and a kaleidoscope of marine life. Visitors can explore this underwater paradise through snorkeling, scuba diving, or taking a scenic boat tour. Cairns provides a launching point for various reef adventures, including visits to popular reef islands and outer reef excursions.

Daintree Rainforest:

North of Cairns lies the Daintree Rainforest, one of the oldest rainforests on the planet. This UNESCO-listed site is a haven for biodiversity, featuring unique flora and fauna, ancient ferns, and crystal-clear streams. Travelers can explore the Daintree on guided walks, river cruises, or ziplining adventures. Mossman Gorge, within the Daintree, is renowned for its stunning landscapes and cultural significance to the local Indigenous communities.

Kuranda Scenic Railway:

For a journey through picturesque landscapes, the Kuranda Scenic Railway offers a memorable experience. Departing from Cairns, the railway winds its way through lush rainforest, steep ravines, and cascading waterfalls. The destination, Kuranda Village, nestled in the rainforest, provides opportunities to explore local markets, wildlife parks, and cultural exhibits. The Skyrail Rainforest Cableway offers an alternative return journey, showcasing expansive views of the rainforest canopy.

Chapter 4: Travel Logistics: Transportation within Australia

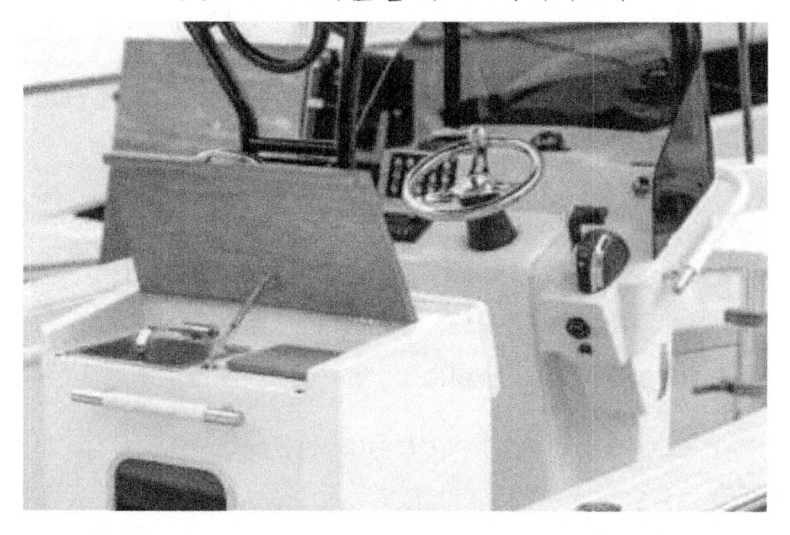

Navigating the vast expanse of Australia requires a thoughtful approach to transportation. The country offers a range of options to suit different preferences and travel styles.

Domestic Flights

Advantages: Australia's major cities are well-connected by domestic flights, offering a quick and efficient way to cover long distances.

Considerations: While convenient, it's essential to book flights in advance, especially during peak travel seasons, and be mindful of baggage allowances.

TRAINS:

Advantages: Australia features long-distance train services, such as the iconic Indian Pacific and The Ghan, providing scenic journeys and a unique way to explore the country.

Considerations: Train travel can be leisurely and immersive, but schedules may be less frequent than other modes of transportation.

BUSES AND COACHES:

Advantages: Bus services connect various regional areas, offering a budget-friendly option for travelers. Coaches also provide long-distance travel with comfort and amenities.

Considerations: Travel times may be longer compared to flights, and schedules may vary based on the route.

4. Rental Cars:

Advantages: Renting a car provides flexibility, especially for exploring regional areas and natural attractions. It allows travelers to set their own pace.

Considerations: Driving long distances requires planning, and adherence to local traffic rules is crucial. Fuel and road conditions should also be considered.

Public Transport in Cities:

Advantages: Major cities like Sydney, Melbourne, and Brisbane have efficient public transportation networks, including trains, buses, and trams.

Considerations: Familiarize yourself with city transport cards or ticketing systems, as well as peak travel times to avoid congestion.

Ride-Sharing Services:

Advantages: Ride-sharing services operate in urban areas, providing a convenient option for short-distance travel.

Considerations: Availability may vary in regional areas, and prices can fluctuate based on demand.

Ferries:

Advantages: In cities like Sydney, ferries offer a scenic way to travel between waterfront locations.

Considerations: Check schedules and routes, as ferry services may be specific to certain areas.

Chapter 5: Accommodation Options

Australia caters to diverse accommodation preferences, ranging from luxurious hotels to budget-friendly options, ensuring there's something for every traveler.

Hotels and Resorts

Advantages: Offer comfort, amenities, and often convenient locations in major cities and tourist areas.

Considerations: Prices vary based on the hotel class and location. Booking in advance, especially during peak seasons, is advisable.

Hostels

Advantages: Budget-friendly option, ideal for solo travelers or those seeking a social atmosphere.

Considerations: Shared dorms or private rooms are available. Some hostels provide communal kitchens and organized activities.

Short-Term Rentals:

Advantages: Platforms like Airbnb offer a variety of accommodations, from entire homes to private rooms.

Considerations: Provides a more local experience. Check reviews and communication with hosts for a smooth stay.

Motels and Motor Inns:

Advantages: Often located along highways, offering convenience for road trips. More affordable than hotels.

Considerations: Facilities may be simpler compared to hotels.

Bed and Breakfasts (B&Bs):

Advantages: Personalized service, often in charming houses. Includes breakfast in the stay.

Considerations: Limited availability in certain areas. Reservations are recommended.

Currency and Banking:

Understanding the currency and banking system is crucial for a seamless financial experience during your stay in Australia.

Currency:

Currency: Australian Dollar (AUD). Coins: 5, 10, 20, 50 cents, and $1, $2. Notes: $5, $10, $20, $50, $100.

Availability: ATMs widely available. Credit and debit cards accepted in most establishments.

Banking:

ATMs: Found in cities, towns, and even remote areas. Check with your bank regarding international withdrawal fees.

Credit Cards: Widely accepted. Visa and MasterCard are commonly used. American Express and Diners Club may have limited acceptance.

Currency Exchange: Available at airports, banks, and currency exchange offices in major cities.

Tipping:

Custom: Tipping is not as common as in some other countries. It is appreciated but not mandatory. Some restaurants may include a service charge.

Mobile Payments: Options: Mobile payment apps like Apple Pay and Google Pay are accepted in many places.

Chapter 6: Australian Cuisine and Dining

Iconic Australian Dishes

Australia's culinary scene reflects its diverse cultural influences and abundant natural resources. From indigenous ingredients to international flavors, here are some iconic

Australian dishes that showcase the country's unique gastronomy:

Vegemite on Toast:

Description: A quintessential Australian breakfast, Vegemite is a yeast extract spread on buttered toast. It has a savory, salty flavor and is often paired with cheese.

Tim Tam Slam:

Description: A beloved Aussie treat, the Tim Tam Slam involves biting off both ends of a chocolate-coated biscuit and using it as a straw to sip a hot beverage like coffee or hot chocolate.

Pavlova:

Description: A meringue-based dessert named after the Russian ballet dancer Anna Pavlova. It's crisp on the outside, light and fluffy on the inside, typically topped with whipped cream and fresh fruits.

Meat Pie:

Description: An Aussie classic, the meat pie consists of flaky pastry filled with minced meat (often beef), gravy, and various seasonings. Often enjoyed with tomato sauce (ketchup).

Barramundi:

Description: A popular Australian fish, barramundi is often grilled or pan-fried and served with a variety of accompaniments, showcasing the country's access to fresh seafood.

Damper:

Description: A traditional Australian bush bread, damper is a simple wheat-based bread traditionally baked in the coals of a campfire. It has a dense texture and is typically enjoyed with butter or golden syrup.

Lamingtons:

Description: A classic Australian dessert, lamingtons are squares of sponge cake coated in a layer of chocolate icing and desiccated coconut. They are often enjoyed with a cup of tea or coffee.

Kangaroo Steak:

Description: Kangaroo meat is lean and rich in flavor. Kangaroo steaks are often grilled or pan-seared and served with native Australian ingredients, showcasing the country's unique culinary offerings.

Flat White:

Description: A popular coffee choice in Australia, the flat white is similar to a latte but with a higher coffee-to-milk ratio. It features espresso with velvety microfoam.

Barramundi:

Description: A popular Australian fish, barramundi is often grilled or pan-fried and served with a variety of accompaniments, showcasing the country's access to fresh seafood.

Chapter 7: Local Food Markets:

Exploring local food markets is a delightful way to experience the diverse and fresh produce that Australia has to offer. Here are some notable markets across the country:

Queen Victoria Market

Melbourne

Highlights: One of the largest open-air markets in the Southern Hemisphere, offering a wide array of fresh produce, gourmet foods, and artisanal products.

Sydney Fish Market (Sydney)

Highlights: A seafood lover's paradise with a vast selection of fresh fish, shellfish, and seafood delicacies. There are also restaurants serving delicious seafood dishes.

Eumundi Markets (Queensland)

Highlights: Known for its vibrant atmosphere, Eumundi Markets feature locally made crafts, fashion, and a diverse range of food stalls offering organic and gourmet treats.

Salamanca Market (Hobart)

Highlights: Located in historic Salamanca Place, this market showcases Tasmanian produce, arts, crafts, and live music. It's a great place to experience the local culture.

Fremantle Markets (Perth)

Highlights: Operating since 1897, Fremantle Markets offer a mix of fresh produce, specialty foods, clothing, and unique handmade items in a lively setting.

Dining Etiquette

Understanding dining etiquette ensures a respectful and enjoyable culinary experience in Australia:

Tipping:

Custom: Tipping is appreciated but not obligatory. It is common to leave around 10% in restaurants if service is not included.

Reservations:

Advisable: Making reservations, especially in popular restaurants, is advisable to secure a table, especially during peak dining hours.

Table Service:

Custom: Table service is standard in restaurants. Waitstaff will guide you through the menu, take orders, and provide assistance.

Cutlery Usage

Etiquette: Use cutlery from the outside in, with the fork on the left and the knife on the right.

When finished, place your cutlery together on the plate at a slight angle.

Wine and Beer

Etiquette: It is acceptable to bring your own wine to some restaurants, but a corkage fee may apply. Australia has a rich wine culture, so exploring local wines is recommended.

Wait for the Host

Custom: Wait for the host or hostess to initiate the start of the meal, including unfolding your napkin and starting to eat.

Casual Atmosphere

Observation: While Australia has its formal dining establishments, the overall dining culture is often casual and relaxed.

Chapter 8: Cultural Experiences

Indigenous Australian Culture

Australia's Indigenous cultures, with a history dating back over 65,000 years, contribute significantly to the nation's rich tapestry. Engaging in cultural experiences provides a profound understanding of the world's oldest living cultures:

Indigenous Art

Description: Explore traditional and contemporary Indigenous art, including paintings, sculptures, and crafts. Each piece often carries deep cultural significance and tells a unique story.

Cultural Festivals and Events

Description: Attend Indigenous cultural festivals and events held throughout the country. These gatherings showcase traditional dance, music, storytelling, and art, providing a vibrant and immersive experience.

Cultural Centers and Museums

Description: Visit Indigenous cultural centers and museums that celebrate and preserve the diverse cultures of Australia's First Nations peoples. Notable examples include the National Museum of Australia in Canberra and the Tjapukai Aboriginal Cultural Park in Cairns.

Dreamtime Stories

Description: Explore Dreamtime stories, the cultural and spiritual narratives of Indigenous Australians. These stories, passed down through generations, explain the creation of the land, animals, and the laws that govern life.

Guided Indigenous Tours:

Description: Participate in guided tours led by Indigenous guides. These tours often include visits to significant cultural sites, bush tucker (native food) experiences, and insights into traditional practices.

Artisan Markets:

Description: Attend markets that showcase Indigenous arts and crafts, allowing you to purchase authentic artworks and handmade items directly from Indigenous artists.

Acknowledgment of Country

Custom: Learn and practice the acknowledgment of country, a way of recognizing and showing respect for the traditional custodians of the land before events or gatherings.

Bush Walks and Cultural Experiences:

Description: Participate in guided bush walks with Indigenous guides who share knowledge about the local flora, fauna, and cultural practices tied to the land.

Language Workshops:

Description: Attend workshops to learn about Indigenous languages. Language is an integral part of cultural identity, and efforts to revive and preserve Indigenous languages are ongoing.

Respectful Engagement

Etiquette: Approach Indigenous experiences with respect and an open mind. Be willing to listen, learn, and appreciate the diversity within Indigenous cultures.

Festivals and Events

Australia hosts a vibrant array of festivals and events that showcase its cultural diversity, arts, and entertainment. Here are some notable celebrations across the country

Sydney Festival (Sydney, NSW):

Description: A multidisciplinary arts festival featuring theater, dance, music, and visual arts, held annually in January. It transforms Sydney into a cultural hub with both free and ticketed events.

Melbourne International Comedy Festival (Melbourne, VIC):

Description: One of the largest comedy festivals globally, featuring stand-up, cabaret, and sketch comedy. It takes place annually from March to April, attracting comedians from around the world.

Vivid Sydney (Sydney, NSW):

Description: An annual light, music, and ideas festival held in Sydney during May and June. The city becomes a canvas for light projections, and there are music performances and discussions on various topics.

WOMADelaide (Adelaide, SA):

Description: A world music and dance festival held annually in Adelaide's Botanic Park. It celebrates global cultural diversity with performances, workshops, and food stalls.

Woodford Folk Festival (Woodford, QLD):

Description: Held over six days and nights at the end of December, this festival in Queensland features music, arts, workshops, and cultural experiences. It is one of the largest folk festivals in the Southern Hemisphere.

Museums and Galleries:

Australia boasts world-class museums and galleries that offer a deep dive into its history, art, and cultural heritage. Here are some noteworthy institutions:

National Gallery of Australia (Canberra, ACT):

Highlights: Home to an extensive collection of Australian and international art, including the famous "Blue Poles" by Jackson Pollock.

Art Gallery of New South Wales (Sydney, NSW):

Highlights: Features a diverse range of Australian, European, and Asian art. The Archibald Prize, an annual portrait competition, is held here.

National Museum of Australia (Canberra, ACT):

Highlights: Showcases Australia's social history, indigenous cultures, and key events. Interactive exhibits provide an engaging experience.

Museum of Old and New Art (MONA) (Hobart, TAS):

Highlights: Located in Tasmania, MONA is known for its avant-garde and controversial contemporary art collection, displayed in an underground space.

Queensland Art Gallery and Gallery of Modern Art (Brisbane, QLD):

Highlights: Combined, these galleries offer a diverse range of Australian and international art. The Asia Pacific Triennial of Contemporary Art is a major event held here.

Australian Museum (Sydney, NSW):

Highlights: Australia's oldest museum, with exhibits on natural history, indigenous cultures, and the country's unique wildlife.

Heide Museum of Modern Art (Melbourne, VIC):

Highlights: Showcases modern and contemporary art in a unique setting. The museum is set within beautiful gardens and sculpture parks.

Chapter 9: Adventure and Outdoor Activities

Hiking in the Blue Mountains

The Blue Mountains, located just outside Sydney, are a haven for outdoor enthusiasts, offering a myriad of hiking trails through lush forests, rugged cliffs, and stunning landscapes. Here's a guide to experiencing the adventure of hiking in the Blue Mountains:

Three Sisters and Echo Point:

Description: Start your adventure at Echo Point, where you can marvel at the iconic Three Sisters rock formation. Several trails, such as the Prince Henry Cliff Walk, offer breathtaking views of these sandstone pillars.

National Pass Trail:

Description: A historic trail that takes you along sheer cliff edges, through lush rainforest, and past cascading waterfalls. It provides a glimpse into the area's coal mining history.

Wentworth Falls Track:

Description: This track takes you to the majestic Wentworth Falls, one of the most beautiful waterfalls in the Blue Mountains. The trail offers various vantage points to appreciate the falls and surrounding scenery.

Govetts Leap to Pulpit Rock:

Description: A challenging yet rewarding hike that takes you to Govetts Leap Lookout for panoramic views, then continues to Pulpit Rock, providing a unique perspective of the Grose Valley.

Grand Canyon Track:

Description: Not to be confused with its American counterpart, the Grand Canyon Track is a stunning circuit that leads you through lush rainforest and past towering sandstone walls. It's known for its diverse plant life and birdwatching opportunities.

National Pass and Wentworth Falls Circuit:

Description: Combining the National Pass and Wentworth Falls Track, this circuit offers a comprehensive exploration of the area. It includes scenic lookouts, waterfalls, and a variety of vegetation.

Sublime Point Lookout to Leura Cascades:

Description: A moderate trail that takes you from Sublime Point Lookout to Leura Cascades. Along the way, you'll encounter eucalyptus forests, sandstone cliffs, and picturesque waterfalls.

Tips for Hiking in the Blue Mountains:

Wear sturdy hiking boots, especially for more challenging trails with uneven terrain.

Carry sufficient water, snacks, and sun protection, as the weather can vary.

Check weather conditions and trail updates before embarking on your hike.

Respect the natural environment and adhere to Leave No Trace principles.

Surfing in Byron Bay

Byron Bay, located on the eastern coast of Australia, is renowned for its stunning beaches and excellent surf conditions. Here's a guide to experiencing the thrill of surfing in Byron Bay:

Main Beach:

Description: Main Beach in Byron Bay is an ideal spot for beginners. The gentle waves and sandy bottom make it a welcoming place to learn how to surf. Numerous surf schools operate in the area, offering lessons for all skill levels.

The Pass:

Description: The Pass is a popular surf break known for its consistent waves. It's suitable for both beginners and experienced surfers. The long, peeling waves make for an enjoyable ride, and the scenic surroundings add to the experience.

Wategos Beach:

Description: Located just north of Cape Byron, Wategos Beach offers a more secluded and relaxed surfing atmosphere. The waves are typically smaller, making it an excellent spot for learners. The picturesque setting adds to the allure.

Tallow Beach:

Description: South of Cape Byron, Tallow Beach is known for its powerful waves, attracting more experienced surfers. The beach is long, providing plenty of space for surfers to find their perfect wave.

Surf Schools:

Recommendation: If you're new to surfing, consider taking lessons from one of the reputable surf schools in Byron Bay. Experienced instructors can provide guidance on technique, safety, and etiquette.

Surfing Events:

Tip: Check if there are any surfing events or competitions happening during your visit. Byron Bay occasionally hosts surf competitions, offering a chance to witness skilled surfers in action.

Sunrise Surf Sessions:

Suggestion: Experience the magic of sunrise while catching early morning waves. The soft hues of the dawn sky combined with the thrill of surfing create a memorable experience.

Wildlife Encounters

Australia is home to a diverse array of wildlife, and encounters with native species are a highlight of any visit. Here are some ways to experience wildlife in and around Byron Bay:

Whale Watching:

Season: From May to November, humpback whales migrate along the coast. Numerous operators in Byron Bay offer whale-watching tours for an up-close view of these majestic creatures.

Cape Byron Walking Track:

Description: Embark on the Cape Byron Walking Track, which leads to the easternmost point of the Australian mainland. Along the way, you may spot dolphins, sea turtles, and various bird species.

Byron Bay Wildlife Sanctuary:

Description: Visit wildlife sanctuaries like the Macadamia Castle or the Byron Bay Wildlife Hospital to encounter native animals such as kangaroos, koalas, and reptiles. Some places offer hands-on experiences.

Dolphin Kayaking Tours:

Experience: Join a guided kayaking tour to explore the coastline and, if you're lucky, encounter dolphins playing in the waves. These tours often provide a unique perspective of Byron Bay's marine life.

Night Vision Walks:

Option: Participate in guided night vision walks to discover the nocturnal wildlife of the region, including possums, flying foxes, and other creatures that come to life after dark.

Snorkeling at Julian Rocks Marine Reserve:

Highlights: Explore the underwater world at Julian Rocks, a marine reserve near Byron Bay.

Encounter sea turtles, rays, and a variety of fish species while snorkeling in this protected area.

Chapter 10: Practical Tips for Travelers:

Traveling to Australia requires some practical considerations to ensure a smooth and enjoyable trip. Here are some tips for travelers:

Voltage and Plugs

Voltage: Australia operates on 230V, and the standard frequency is 50Hz. Check if you need a power adapter or converter for your electronic devices.

Emergency Services:

Contact: In case of emergencies, dial 000 for immediate assistance. This number connects you to police, fire, and ambulance services.

Health Insurance:

Recommendation: It's advisable to have comprehensive travel insurance covering health emergencies and unexpected events during your stay in Australia.

Transportation Cards:

City Travel: In major cities like Sydney and Melbourne, consider getting a transportation card (Opal in Sydney, Myki in Melbourne) for convenient use on buses, trains, and trams.

Sun Protection:

Essential: Australia has high UV levels. Wear sunscreen, a hat, and sunglasses to protect yourself from the strong sun, especially if you're engaging in outdoor activities.

Currency Exchange:

Options: While credit cards are widely accepted, having some local currency (Australian Dollars) for small expenses is recommended. Currency exchange services are available at airports and banks.

Wi-Fi and SIM Cards:

Connectivity: Wi-Fi is common in urban areas, but having a local SIM card can be useful for staying connected, especially in regional areas.

Water Safety:

Caution: If you're swimming at beaches or in natural bodies of water, be aware of local conditions and follow safety guidelines. Australia's coastlines can have strong currents.

Time Zones and Weather

Time Zones:

✓ Eastern Standard Time (EST): UTC+10
✓ Australian Eastern Daylight Time (AEDT): UTC+11 (observed during daylight saving time, usually from October to April)

Weather:

Seasons: Australia's seasons are the opposite of the Northern Hemisphere. Summer is from December to February, autumn from March to May, winter from June to August, and spring from September to November.

Diverse Climates:

Variation: Australia has diverse climates. Coastal areas are generally milder, while the interior (Outback) can experience extreme temperatures. Check the weather for your specific destinations.

Rainfall:

Varies: Northern regions (Queensland, Northern Territory) have a wet and dry season. Southern regions (Victoria, New South Wales) experience more consistent rainfall throughout the year.

Packing Essentials:

Considerations: Pack according to the climate of your destinations. Lightweight clothing, swimwear, and sun protection items are essential, especially in summer. For cooler months or southern regions, bring layers.

Check Local Forecasts:

Preparation: Weather conditions can vary across the vast country. Check local forecasts for each destination, especially if you're traveling between regions.

Chapter II: Safety Tips:

10 Tips to Drive Safe in Australia

Ensuring your safety while traveling in Australia involves a combination of general precautions and awareness of specific factors. Here are some safety tips for your trip:

Emergency Services:

Dial: In case of emergencies, dial 000 for immediate assistance. This number connects you to police, fire, and ambulance services.

Health Precautions:

Insurance: Have comprehensive travel insurance covering health emergencies and unexpected events. Familiarize yourself with medical facilities in the areas you'll be visiting.

Wildlife Caution:

Respect: Australia is home to unique wildlife. Admire animals from a safe distance and be aware of the potential presence of snakes in certain areas.

Water Safety:

Be Informed: If swimming in the ocean, check for surf conditions and follow any warnings. Swim between the flags at patrolled beaches. Be cautious of strong currents.

Sun Protection:

UV Awareness: Australia has high UV levels. Wear sunscreen, a hat, and sunglasses to protect yourself from the strong sun, especially if engaging in outdoor activities.

Weather Preparedness:

Check Forecasts: Australia's weather can be diverse. Check local forecasts for your destinations and pack accordingly, especially if traveling between regions.

Transportation Safety:

Follow Rules: Whether driving, using public transportation, or participating in adventure activities, follow safety guidelines and regulations. If driving, be mindful of wildlife on roads, particularly in rural areas.

Respect Local Customs:

Cultural Awareness: Respect the diverse cultures in Australia. Be aware of Indigenous cultural sites and follow any guidelines or restrictions in these areas.

Communication and Connectivity

Mobile Networks:

Coverage: Australia has extensive mobile network coverage. Check with your mobile provider about international roaming or consider getting a local SIM card for better rates.

Wi-Fi Availability:

Urban Areas: Wi-Fi is commonly available in urban areas, including hotels, cafes, and public spaces. Many accommodations offer free or paid Wi-Fi services.

Emergency Contact Information:

Note Down: Keep a note of emergency contact information, including local emergency services and the contact details of your country's embassy or consulate in Australia.

Navigation Apps:

Useful: Download navigation apps for your smartphone to help with directions, especially if you plan to explore on foot or use public transportation.

Emergency Alerts:

Stay Informed: Be aware of emergency alert systems that provide information about severe weather, bushfires, or other incidents. Follow local authorities' advice.

Communication Language:

English: English is the official language. However, due to Australia's multicultural society, you may encounter people who speak various languages, especially in urban areas.

Internet Cafes:

Options: In addition to Wi-Fi, internet cafes are available in some areas if you need access to computers and the internet.

Chapter 12: Sustainable Travel Practices

Traveling sustainably helps minimize your environmental impact and contributes to the preservation of natural and cultural resources. Here are some sustainable travel practices to consider during your trip to Australia:

Reduce Single-Use Plastics:

Reusable Items: Bring a reusable water bottle, shopping bag, and utensils to minimize reliance on single-use plastics. Refill water at water stations or carry a reusable bottle to reduce plastic waste.

Stay in Eco-Friendly Accommodations:

Certifications: Choose accommodations with recognized eco-certifications or those implementing sustainable practices. Look for hotels that prioritize energy efficiency, waste reduction, and water conservation.

Conserve Water and Energy:

Hotel Practices: Conserve water by reusing towels and linens in hotels. Turn off lights, air conditioning, and electronics when not in use to reduce energy consumption.

Support Local Products and Markets:

Local Economy: Purchase locally-made products and souvenirs to support local economies and reduce the carbon footprint associated with imported goods.

Respect Wildlife:

Observation Only: Observe wildlife in their natural habitats without disturbing or feeding them. Choose responsible wildlife tours that prioritize the well-being of animals and their habitats.

Responsible Tourism:

Cultural Respect: Respect local cultures, traditions, and customs. Engage with communities in a meaningful and respectful way, contributing positively to their economies.

Mindful Transportation:

Public Transport: Use public transportation, walk, or cycle whenever possible. In larger cities, efficient public transport systems are available. Consider carbon offset programs for flights.

Leave No Trace:

Nature Conservation: Follow the principles of Leave No Trace by not littering, staying on designated paths, and avoiding damage to natural environments. Leave cultural and historical sites as you found them.

Eco friendly Activities

Nature Conservation Tours:

Guided Tours: Join guided tours focused on nature conservation, such as rainforest walks or coastal clean-up activities. These experiences contribute to the preservation of natural habitats.

Snorkeling in Marine Protected Areas:

Protected Sites: Enjoy snorkeling or diving in marine protected areas, contributing to the conservation of coral reefs and marine ecosystems.

National Park Exploration:

Guided Walks: Explore national parks with guided eco-friendly walks that educate participants on local flora, fauna, and conservation efforts.

Bird Watching and Wildlife Safaris:

Observation: Participate in bird watching or wildlife safaris with trained guides who prioritize animal welfare and habitat preservation.

Community-Based Tourism:

Local Initiatives: Support community-based tourism initiatives that empower local communities, showcasing their traditions and crafts while contributing to sustainable development.

Sustainable Food Experiences:

Farm-to-Table: Choose restaurants and food experiences that prioritize locally sourced, seasonal, and sustainable ingredients. Support businesses committed to ethical and eco-friendly practices.

Educational Eco-Tours:

Learning Experiences: Engage in eco-tours that provide educational insights into the local ecosystems, conservation efforts, and environmental challenges.

Volunteer Opportunities:

Conservation Projects: Explore volunteer opportunities with conservation projects or environmental organizations, contributing your time and skills to local sustainability efforts.

Responsible Wildlife Tourism

Tourism Australia

When engaging in wildlife tourism, it's crucial to prioritize responsible and ethical practices to ensure the well-being of animals and their habitats. Here are guidelines for responsible wildlife tourism:

Choose Accredited Sanctuaries:

Research: Opt for wildlife sanctuaries and rehabilitation centers that are accredited by recognized organizations. These facilities prioritize the welfare of animals and adhere to ethical standards.

No Interference with Wild Animals:

Observe Only: Avoid engaging in activities that involve direct contact with wild animals. Observe them in their natural habitats without causing disturbance or stress.

Wildlife Conservation Tours:

Support Initiatives: Participate in wildlife conservation tours that contribute to the protection and preservation of endangered species and their ecosystems.

Avoid Selfies with Wildlife:

Respect Distance: Refrain from taking selfies or attempting to touch wild animals. Maintain a safe and respectful distance to minimize stress and disruption.

Say No to Animal Performances:

Avoid Shows: Choose not to participate in activities that involve animals performing tricks or behaviors. Such practices may involve cruelty and exploitation.

Educate Yourself

Learn About Wildlife: Educate yourself about the species you encounter. Understanding their behavior and natural habitats enhances your wildlife experience and encourages responsible behavior.

Responsible Snorkeling and Diving:

Coral Conservation: When snorkeling or diving, practice responsible behavior by not touching coral reefs or marine life. Choose operators committed to coral conservation.

Report Unethical Practices:

Speak Up: If you witness unethical practices or animal mistreatment, report them to the authorities or the management of the facility. Advocate for responsible wildlife tourism.

Reduce Reuse Recycle

Reduce Single-Use Plastics:

Reusable Items: Bring a reusable water bottle, shopping bag, and utensils to reduce reliance on single-use plastics. Refill water at water stations to minimize plastic waste.

Choose Eco-Friendly Accommodations:

Certifications: Stay in accommodations that implement eco-friendly practices, such as waste reduction, energy efficiency, and water conservation.

Pack Light and Wisely:

Minimize Waste: Pack only what you need and avoid excessive packaging. Dispose of waste responsibly, using recycling facilities when available.

Use Public Transportation:

Reduce Emissions: Opt for public transportation, walk, or cycle to minimize your carbon footprint. Use eco-friendly transportation options when available.

Support Sustainable Products:

Local and Sustainable: Choose products made from sustainable materials and support local artisans. Avoid purchasing items that contribute to deforestation or harm wildlife.

Dispose of Waste Properly:

Follow Guidelines: Dispose of waste in designated bins and follow local recycling guidelines. Be mindful of waste management practices in different regions.

Conserve Water and Energy:

Hotel Practices: Conserve water and energy by reusing towels and turning off lights and electronics when not in use. Follow eco-friendly practices in accommodations.

Participate in Clean-Up Initiatives:

Community Engagement: Join beach clean-up initiatives or community-led efforts to reduce litter and plastic pollution in natural areas.

Please! Please!! Please!!!

I assume that if you have read this far in the book, you have at least somewhat enjoyed it. These days, the widely recognized Amazon review is used to evaluate books. Would you mind taking a few minutes to assist me win a bet with a speaker friend of mine that I can get more reviews than she does? I'm not sure if this is for you.

It would only make sense to tell you how else we could support one another while I'm asking.

Having the intelligence to hold all publishing rights, my team and I can assist you directly with large orders of this book, saving you a tonne of money. We may also alter the cover to better represent your brand, and we could even be willing to modify the examples to better reflect your particular sector. I provide this personalization to my speaking customers, and I would be happy to talk about doing the same for you. Kindly send Ben an email at benjamite2019@gmail.com so that we can arrange a time to talk.

Pls gist me about your journey in my email. Safe Journey...

Printed in Great Britain
by Amazon